Poem for a Stranger

Abigail Rose

Presentation by *BookLeaf Publishing*

Web: www.bookleafpub.com

E-mail: info@bookleafpub.com

ISBN: 9789358737967

First edition 2023

*Poem for a Stranger is dedicated to all of
the people who trusted me with their
stories, and to all of the strangers with
stories yet to be told.*

ACKNOWLEDGEMENT

A huge thank you to everyone who has supported me from the sidelines through this project, and to BookLeaf Publishing for making this long time dream a reality!

PREFACE

My name is Abigail Rose, and I am a storyteller. Through years of searching for great stories, I have learned that every person has a story to tell, and that even the seemingly insignificant parts of life can offer some of the most meaningful stories and lessons. Through this project, I hope to find, and share stories that otherwise might be lost by time. Every day, for 21 days, I searched for a stranger. Every day, I approached someone who I'd never met, and who had never met me. I told each of them the same thing. My name is Abigail Rose, and my project is called "Poem for a Stranger". I would like to hear and write your story, if I could have a few minutes of your time. All you need to do is talk. It can be about anything, your first love, your first heartbreak, a moment you were proud of yourself, or ashamed, a good memory, a passion of yours, a time when you were afraid, or something else entirely. I will then take what I have learned from you, and write it in the form of a poem. This poem will be titled with your name if you are comfortable sharing, or simply titled "anonymous" if you aren't. If they agreed to share with me, I did just that. I hope that whoever may read this can connect to these people as I have, meeting them as strangers, and forming a connection of vulnerability that may make us all feel less alone.

Arin

They were sitting in a ring,
In a cabin,
Somewhere miles from home
In a state filled with ancient
And wild woods

They each had a drink in hand,
And the stars floated
On the surface of the evening sky

As the night drew on,
The drinks began to blur the lines
Between reality
And the game

Characters and identities
Melted and melded
Until each of them was
A valiant hero, or
Mischievous mage, or
Kindhearted elf
And their daring adventure
Felt as real as
The lives they were escaping
For the week

The revelry coursed on
Until, eventually,
The drinks made
The adventure impossible,
And the night persisted
With friendships forged
From years of trials and tribulations,
Both real and fabricated,

When, finally,
Foggy minds gave way to sleep,
A new day rose
With the promise of quests, and
Brotherhood everlasting

Julia

She was the third
Of three sisters,
Raised on crabapples
And thin mountain air.
She spent her weekends
With her sisters, or outside,
Marveling at the landscape,
Blanketed in glimmering ivory
At all times of the year

Then, years later,
She traded snowfalls for sandbanks,
White capped mountains
For a city
Sprawled under a brilliant sun
Whose rays fell to the ground
On even the cloudiest days

The openness of the land
Made life feel limitless,
But the thousands of people
Couldn't replace the sisters she'd left behind,
And the white sand beaches
Didn't compare to
The crystals of freshly fallen snow

Back home

Few changes come without joy, though,
Because even hundreds of miles from home,
A tortoiseshell kitten
With eyes that loved nothing more
Than to adore her,
And a name,
Misty,
Like the mist that hung
Over the mountains of Vermont,
Could make any place feel like home.

Anonymous

The water was
As much a part of her
As the blood
Flowing through her veins

After plunging
Into the depths of
Cold water,
Breaking the surface was
Indescribable
Like the air she was breathing was
Purer,
Lighter.

The methodic flicks
Of her legs and arms
Sent her gliding through the water
As if she had taken flight
And even as her lungs
Ached for the air above
Her heart
Ached to stay

And watching the rainbow hues
Of the dusk sunlight

Glint on the tops of
Ocean waves,
Felt like finding something
In herself
A freedom
That was strongest when
She could feel the water
Caressing her skin

But suddenly,
The water that had always
Soothed her aches
Ignited a flame
Across her skin
The place that had always
Felt like home
Was inaccessible

She had to watch the others
Sliding through the water,
Getting faster and stronger,
All while the one thing
That gave her peace
Had been stripped from her

Noah

His dad worked
From sundown to sunup
And would return
In the early morning hours
With food for his son

They'd watch movies together
And eat a sweet breakfast,
Until his dad dozed off
But it didn't matter
If he was awake
Or not
It was enough that
He was there

He'd write stories
Because he could create
Anything
Be anyone

He'd write about his family,
His father who stayed awake
Just to spend time with him,
The brother who had already left
For the military

With just a pen and paper,
A lonely day
In a diner by the beach
Became an
Endless adventure

A boy became a god,
Creating new worlds
And guiding
Heroes and villains
Through the mightiest of triumphs
And the most devastating defeats

One day perhaps
He would live somewhere secluded,
Digging up treasures
Of people long gone
And imagining
The stories that they
Might hold

Anna

The idea that
You could create something
So incredible
Out of something so simple
Gives her hope
Like if grapes,
Given enough time,
And a little push,
Can become wine,
Then perhaps one person
Can create change
One idea could
Inspire generations of
Sustainability
Someone with enough drive
Could create what is needed
For the Earth to thrive

And the fact that
Something we made so long ago,
A product of years of
Innovation and change
Can still be appreciated today,
Reminds her that perhaps,
The products of her work

Which may be seen as mundane in her time,
Could be celebrated for their value
Viewed as a masterpiece,
And a beautiful product of history
In the years to come

She knows that
Time is transformative

Anonymous

For her, home is green
It's filled with trees
And rolling hills

The mountains poke up
Out of the ground
Like curious heads

Her father,
The most adventurous in the family,
Likes to climb those stone faces
And she follows along,
Watching him climb
To the highest point
For the sake of the most beautiful views

But for everything
Her world has to offer,
She can't help but be captivated
By the worlds she finds
In ink on paper

She trades the rocky giants
For dragons and magic,
Her green home,

For a world which she can create

For what is sweeter than that
Which we do not have?

Robin

Teaching others the skills
They need
To make a way for themselves in the world
Is her gift
To her students

And when tragedy struck
In her own life,
She left her place as a guide
And guardian
Of young minds
For a time

But though grief
Is a lifelong process,
She continued to give herself
And her knowledge to
Those who wanted a life
As fulfilled as hers
Is and had been

Even with a part of her gone,
She honored him
In every way she could
She honored him through her life

And her work
She honored his memory
Through her love for the family
And life
They had built together

And one day,
She hoped to see his homeland,
To see the birthplace of his ancestors
And to spread some of his ashes
In Hungary
To bring him home

For his home was both
With her,
And with the ones
Who came before them
Whose choices
Had allowed them
To have such a beautiful life
With each other

The family that they
Built was her pride and joy.
A daughter,
And a son, who had given her
Two beautiful grandchildren,
Whose faces held pieces of
The of the man she loves

Her daughter was an inventor
Who spun words into worlds
And creations so full of life

The man she married
Was a writer too,
And their words were their gift to the world,
Just as knowledge was her mother's

And her mother knew
The value that their gifts held
She'd say
Anything that you love,
You should be able to do everyday

And those things that they loved,
Gave others the courage
To create
And share their wisdom,
Just as these incredible women
Had done

Kaleb

Just like the rest of us,
Quarantine came with its costs
But for him,
The cost was far greater than isolation
The man who had taught him
What it meant to be a leader,
How to grow
And become the version of himself
That he could be most proud of
Died that year

So years later,
When he had completed his journey
In growth and leadership
It felt right
To commemorate that man,
And the men before him
Who gave so much
Of themselves to others
And helped generations of boys
Become men with compassion
And drive for bettering their community

He, along with some
Like minded scouts

Spent weeks, in the sun
Or in the rain,
Creating a space
To be dedicated to
Those men whose passion for teaching
And compassionate natures
Had helped them find
Their place in the world

Aya

She grew up
Oceans away,
And traveled
To a foreign place
To see the land
The sun shone on
During moonless nights back home

Some things were pleasant
Like the temperament
Of the other students,
While other things were strange
And unsettling
Like the gaps in the bathroom doors
That people would peer into
Before opening the door
And the food
Was a poor imitation
Of the foods she knew and loved
Even the foods
Inspired by Japan
Tasted foreign and strange

Some things though
Never changed,

Like the way the drumbeats
In dance music
Matched her heartbeat
Until she felt like
Perhaps the music
Was coming from somewhere
Inside her

Ryouto

Everything was so different
From the life he knew at home
Cars scurried around the street
Like frantic mice,
And there was no train to take him
From place to place

The food was unusual
Sometimes unpleasant,
And nothing compared to
Fresh, hot ramen
Which warmed his insides
And felt like eating comfort itself

The buildings looked
Like formidable giants
Clad in marble and stone
So unlike the organic shapes
He'd see at home
But they had their own beauty
And their history,
The stories that they told,
Made them all the more captivating

The people he met,

Were so kind,
They were always welcoming
And generous,
But also understood
That sometimes
Being alone had its own sense of comfort

So, even far from home,
He felt like he belonged

Elias

He would visit the beach
Every day
Just to be near the water
And the open sky

He found that the ocean
Was most beautiful
At sunrise,
When a new day
Rose with the sun,
Shining rosy light
Across the waves

The waves themselves
Seemed to be waking
With the sun,
Their rhythm growing
Cheerier,
Like the ocean
Was wishing him a good day

The water allowed him
To be live the way he wanted to
He had been bigger,
And hated the way it made him feel

And the way others
Made him feel

But the water held him up,
Same as it did everyone else,
Like he was weightless

And swimming made him strong,
And transformed his body
As if he was embarking on a new
State of existence

Claudia

She loved her work,
Giving kids the opportunity
To have fun,
Regardless of
If their parents could pay

She met kids from
Every walk of life,
And for as much as
They learned from her
She learned from them

They helped her find
Her passion

She wanted to be an advocate for them,
But more importantly,
Teach them to advocate for themselves,
Because a sharp mind
With a decisive tongue
Can accomplish
More than most think

To give them the ability
To speak for themselves,

Is to give them freedom
To flourish as individuals

Anonymous

He grew up
By the beach,
And gathered
A group of friends
Along the way

He would play
Board games,
Strategizing,
Vying for the win,
But ultimately,
The allure of the games
Was the time spent
With others

Winning gave
Temporary satisfaction,
Like taking a bite of rich food,
But the camaraderie
And friendships
Filled him up like a hot meal

He, with a group of friends
Traveled the world,

In Munich,
They could travel
Anywhere
On foot,
Or by bike,
And following
Their own path
In such a way
Was a unique
Freedom

Sasha

Her partner fit
Against her
Like they were once one,
And had been cleaved apart
So that they could
Find each other,
And a sense of belonging

Their head could rest
Right under her chin,
And holding them
Was like finding
A missing piece
Of herself

They had grown up
Seeing the world,
Experiencing its beauty
Firsthand

And though
She had never dared
To dream of
A life like that,
They made it seem

Possible

She wanted
That kind of life,
One full of beauty
And new experiences,
But she knew
That it would be all the better
Because she had
Someone to share it with

Madison

She grew up
In a small town
Where everyone she loved
Was close by

She would go to church
Every sunday
Just like she had
For as long as she
Could remember

There was comfort
In the familiarity
And the certainty
Knowing nothing would ever
Change there

But she knew
There was more
Out there for her
Somewhere

So she packed her things
And found a place to settle,
Hours away

The city she found
Was bigger than
Anything she'd ever known
And so much changed

But some things
Stayed the same
She still went to church
Every Sunday
And she still loved
Her home
And all the people in it

Luke

Every morning,
He would wake
While the stars still
Spilled across the sky

The job was always the same,
Yet still unexpected
The ocean was
A constantly changing constant
The same ocean
He worked on
Every day,
But with a different temperament

Every day,
A new group,
New people
With new stories,
New personalities,
New goals

And the fish themselves
Were never the same
Some days,
They were gullible,

Taking every piece
Of tasty bait,
Trusting a trap

Other days,
They fought back,
For though it was natural
That they be used to sustain
Other life,
Their instincts led them
To fight for their own
With everything they had

Shannon

She knew
That he was
Her person.
He knew the
Parts of her
That she kept hidden,
And loved her
Ever the more for them

They were
Soulmates,
But not in the way
That their souls matched,
It was as if their souls
Had once been one,
And that soul was torn apart

So that when those pieces
Met again,
They could find
Within each other
All the parts of themselves
They'd been missing

They changed each other,

Because their love
Made them more of themselves
Like finding the other
Was all it took to become
Who they were meant to be

A missed opportunity
For her,
Gave way for him to
Become part of her life,
So the sting of disappointment
Was always soothed by
Thankfulness for his presence
In her life

Even when
They needed to be apart
To grow and heal
As the two people they were,
Their love was never in question

So she began making
One thousand paper cranes
To exchange for a wish,
And as soon as he saw them,
He knew what that wish would be
And something inside him
Was dreaming of that same
Future together

So he sat with her,
And made a crane,
Because though it
Was her wish to make,
It was his too,
So it only felt right
That they take a step together
To make that wish come true

Jordan

He could feel
A face
In a lump of clay
Waiting to be molded
Waiting to be made
And it seemed a tragedy
Not to let face
In the clay
Exist somewhere
Outside his mind

He hoped one day
To sculpt from marble
A masterpiece
That flowed gently
Like the sea over a stone

He would wait
As long as it may take
For the form
Within the marble
To find its way out

And perhaps
One day

Paint a statue
Into his skin,
Where it would have
Movement
And a life of its own

Ishaia

She would stand
In the grass,
Letting the dew
Pass to her feet,
Like little jewels

The wind
Would brush across
The field, making the blades of grass
Sway and dance along with her

She would twirl
With the wind,
Allowing it to
Guide her movements
For there were
No rules to follow,
Just passion
And the wind
To pull beautiful
Fluid movements
From the part of her mind
Made for creation

And with her feet

On the ground,
And the grass tickling her toes,
It felt like the spinning earth
Was dancing alongside her

Drew

His heart was broken
And every part of him
That had been filled
With memories of her
And love for her
Was replaced with regrets

It seeped through his mind
Filling all the cracks
In his thoughts

Any time he had a moment
To think, the regrets
Would come rushing back
Like a tidal wave only held at bay
By distractions

He wanted to be
True to himself,
But that seemed impossible
When he wasn't even sure
Who he was

And waking up miserable
Every day

Made it hard to imagine
That there was a life
To be lived without regrets

Even when he
Told himself that he accepted
The past, the regrets
Persisted
It seemed that maybe,
Those regrets were the
Only thing
That would never leave him

Anonymous

When she left home,
She didn't go far,
But it was far enough
That by the time
She came home again
Everything had changed

Everything in her life
Was constantly moving,
But things at home
Didn't stand still
And wait for her to return

It was like her home
Had moved on
When she moved out
But no matter how much
It changed,
Home was still home

She began taking
Autumn walks on the beach
Where the cool breeze
Made the air smell salty
And fresh

But if she had the time
And the means
She would take
Her whole family back home
To Illinois
Where everything was cozy
And comfortable
Where Mamaw still lived
Because home was still home
For her too

To the city her parents
Met in, and grew up together
The place that felt safest,
Another kind of home